MEXICAN COOKING

Designed by Claire Leighton
Food photography by Peter Barry
Recipes styled by Jacqueline Bellefontaine
Edited by Jillian Stewart
Incidental photography: FPG International,
   Roger Hicks and Frances E. Schultz

2710 Mexican Cooking
This edition published in 1997 by CLB
Distributed in the U.S.A. by BHB International, Inc.
30 Edison Drive, Wayne, New Jersey 07470
© 1992 CLB International
All rights reserved
Printed and bound in Singapore
ISBN 1-85833-676-7

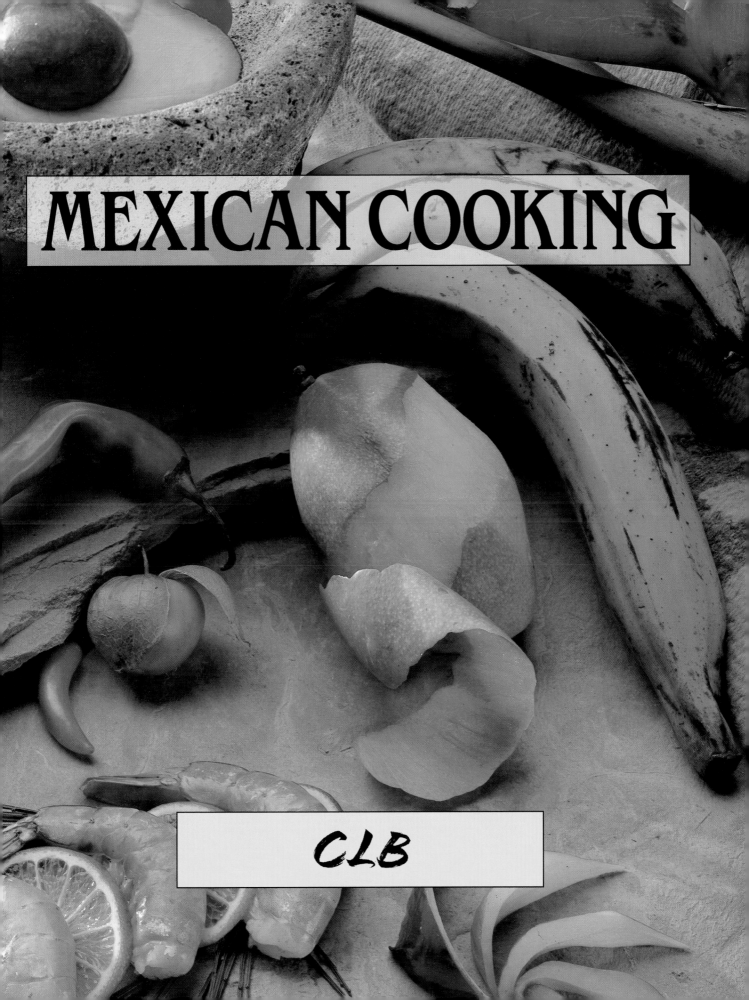

MEXICAN COOKING

CLB

INTRODUCTION

When the Spanish arrived in Mexico they found a wealth of native food that had been part of the Aztec Indians' diet for hundreds of years. Tomatoes, avocados, pineapples, chilies and cocoa were all growing in Mexico and were taken back to Spain by the conquistadors. These products are still important in Mexican cooking today.

Because Mexico shares a common border with the United States, Mexican food has been popular here for a long time. What began as simply a craze for tacos has widened into an appreciation for some of Mexico's finest dishes. The growing popularity of Mexican cuisine is hardly surprising; it is colorful, tasty and exotic. And for those who like it hot, there are numerous spicy dishes. In Mexico, as in many other hot countries, the addition of spices acts as a preservative and stimulates appetites flagging in the heat. But just because food is spicy, it need not be very hot. Cumin, coriander and cinnamon are favorite choices in Mexico and these spices lend their fragrance and flavor without bringing tears to the eyes!

Certain recipes are used frequently in Mexican cooking. Two that we have included are Taco Sauce and Guacamole. Taco sauce in particular is featured in many recipes as a topping or a sauce. Guacamole is an avocado appetizer that is so simple to prepare that you can make it any time, to serve as a first course or with drinks like a Margarita or Tequila Sunrise.

If any one ingredient really symbolizes Mexican cooking, it is the tortilla. In Mexico, tortillas in one form or another appear at every meal. Even if they are not an integral part of a recipe they are served as an accompaniment, even with eggs at breakfast. There are two types of tortillas, each made with different flours. Corn tortillas are made with a fine corn flour, and although they are a little more difficult to make, they are the most popular choice in Mexico. In the northern part of the country, however, wheat is commonly grown so tortillas are more often made with wheat flour. These are easy to make and more pliable, so they are easier to use in recipes. Since they are the foundation of so many of our dishes, we have included a recipe.

The use of cocoa powder in savory dishes may seem like a startling idea, but don't be put off. It gives a depth of color and flavor to meat dishes without making them taste of chocolate. Spanish settlers in Mexico first used the plentiful cocoa bean in their cooking, adapting it to both sweet and savory dishes. While the Spanish also introduced sugar and milk to the cuisine, desserts have not become overly popular in Mexico. Fresh fruit in exotic combinations is still the favorite.

Over the past few years more and more prepared ingredients for Mexican cooking have appeared on the market. But, there is fun to be had in cooking this colorful and exciting cuisine in the traditional way, too. Mexican food may seem exotic, but you won't need any special equipment or great skill to prepare these dishes. And with our easy-to-follow recipes, Mexican cooking couldn't be easier or tastier.

Right: Mexico is a deeply religious country and every town, as well as the smallest village, is dominated by its church.

Chili Vegetable Soup

Preparation Time: about 20 minutes **Cooking Time:** 20 minutes **Serves:** 4

A simple-to-make and delicious soup that makes a light first course.

Ingredients
1 tbsp oil
1 onion, chopped
4oz canned whole green chilies, quartered
4 cups chicken stock
1 large potato, peeled and cut into short strips

Full quantity Taco Sauce recipe
1 tbsp lime juice
Tortilla chips and lime slices to garnish
Salt

Heat the oil in a large saucepan and sauté the onion until translucent. Add the green chilies, stock, potato and taco sauce. Cover the pan and simmer soup for 20 minutes. Stir in the lime juice and add salt. Serve in individual bowls with tortilla chips. Cut a thin slice of lime to float in each bowl of soup.

Mexico is very mountainous so any low-lying areas are intensively farmed.

Guacamole

Preparation Time: about 25 minutes **Serves:** 8

This is one of Mexico's most famous dishes. It is delicious as a first course on its own or as an ingredient in other recipes.

Ingredients

1 medium onion, finely chopped
1 clove garlic, crushed
Grated rind and juice of ½ lime
½ quantity Taco Sauce recipe
3 large avocados

1 tbsp chopped fresh coriander
Pinch salt
Coriander leaves to garnish
1 package tortilla chips

Mix the onion, garlic, rind and juice of lime and the taco sauce together in a large mixing bowl. Cut the avocados in half lengthwise. Twist the halves gently in opposite directions to separate. Hit the stone with a large, sharp knife and twist the knife to remove the stone.

Place the avocado halves cut side down on a chopping board. Lightly score the skin lengthwise and gently pull back to peel. Alternatively, scoop out avocado flesh with a spoon, scraping the skin well. Chop the avocado roughly and immediately place in the bowl with the onion and lime. Use a potato masher to break up the avocado until almost smooth. Do not over-mash. Season with salt and stir in the chopped coriander. Spoon into a serving bowl and garnish with coriander leaves. Surround the bowl with tortilla chips for dipping.

Top: a well-laden *burro* plods along with its quota of firewood.

Shrimp Acapulco

Preparation Time: about 15 minutes **Cooking Time:** 20-25 minutes **Serves:** 4

This makes a stylish appetizer or a quickly prepared snack. Make the bread slices smaller to serve with cocktails.

Ingredients

4 slices bread, crusts removed
6 tbsps softened butter
1 cup cooked and peeled shrimp
½ tsp chili powder
¼ tsp paprika
¼ tsp cumin
Salt and pepper
Watercress to garnish

Cut the bread slices in half and spread with 2 tbsps butter. Butter both sides sparingly. Place the bread on a baking sheet and cook in a preheated 350°F oven for 10-15 minutes until golden brown. Keep warm. Melt the remaining butter in a small pan and add the shrimp, spices and seasoning and stir well. Heat through completely and spoon on top of the bread slices. Garnish with watercress and serve hot.

Top: plowing with an ox in the traditional manner in central Mexico.

Moyettes

Preparation Time: about 15 minutes **Cooking Time:** about 15-20 minutes
Serves: 4

While these sandwiches seem like lunch fare, they are very popular for breakfast in Mexico.

Ingreients
4 crusty rolls
2 tbsps butter or margarine
8oz canned refried beans

2 green onions, chopped
4 tbsps grated Tilsit cheese

Cut the rolls in half and scoop out some of the inside to make a hollow. Soften the butter and spread on both sides of the rolls. Fill the rolls with the refried beans. Sprinkle with the onion and top with the grated cheese. Place the rolls on a baking sheet and cook in a preheated 325°F oven for 15-20 minutes, or until the cheese has melted and the beans are hot. Serve immediately.

Top: Guanajuato contains some of Mexico's most beautiful colonial architecture.

Beef and Bean Soup

Preparation Time: about 20 minutes **Cooking Time:** about 50 minutes **Serves:** 4

In Mexico, the day's main meal is eaten at around 2.00 pm and this soup is a popular appetizer.

Ingredients

1 large onion, peeled and finely chopped
2 sticks celery, chopped
1 red pepper, seeded and finely chopped
2 tbsps oil
1 generous cup ground beef
6 tomatoes, peeled, seeded and chopped

15oz can refried beans
1 tsp ground cumin
1 tsp chili powder
1 tsp garlic powder or paste
Pinch cinnamon and cayenne pepper
2 cups beef stock
Salt and pepper

Fry the onion, celery and pepper in the oil in a large saucepan until softened. Add the beef and fry over medium heat until well browned. Add the tomatoes and refried beans with the spices, garlic and seasoning and mix well. Stir in the stock and bring to the boil. Cover and simmer gently for 30 minutes, stirring occasionally. Pour the soup into a blender or food processor and puree. The soup will be quite thick and not completely smooth. Adjust the seasoning and serve with tortilla chips. Top with sour cream if desired.

Children play in a quiet courtyard near the Municipal Palace in Zacatecas.

Flour Tortillas

Preparation Time: about 60 minutes **Cooking Time:** about 5 minutes **Makes:** 12

Tortillas made with wheat instead of corn are traditional in Northern Mexico. Flour tortillas are easier to make and use than the corn variety.

Ingredients
1lb all-purpose or whole-wheat flour   6 tbsps lard
1 tbsp salt   1 cup hot water

Sift flour and salt into a mixing bowl and rub in the lard until the mixture resembles fine breadcrumbs. Mix in the water gradually to form a soft, pliable dough. Whole-wheat flour may need more water. Knead on a well-floured surface until smooth and no longer sticky. Cover with a damp tea towel. Cut off about 3 tbsps of dough at a time, keeping the rest covered. Knead into a ball. Roll the ball of dough out into a very thin circle with a floured rolling pin. Cut into a neat round using a 10-inch plate as a guide. Continue until all the dough is used. Stack the tortillas as you make them, flouring each one well to prevent sticking. Cover with a clean kitchen towel.

    Heat a heavy-based frying pan and carefully place in a tortilla. Cook for about 10 seconds per side. Stack and keep covered until all are cooked. Use according to chosen recipe.

Brightly colored boats await another day's fishing for marlin and red snapper.

Taco Sauce

Preparation Time: 15-20 minutes **Cooking Time:** 8-10 minutes **Makes:** ½ pint

This basic recipe has many uses in Mexican cooking – sauce, topping, dip or as an ingredient to give a dish extra flavor.

Ingredients

1 tbsp oil
1 onion, diced
1 green pepper, diced
½-1 red or green chili pepper
½ tsp ground cumin

½ tsp ground coriander
½ clove garlic, crushed
Pinch salt, pepper and sugar
14oz canned tomatoes
Tomato paste (optional)

Heat the oil in a heavy-based saucepan and, when hot, add the onion and pepper. Cook slowly to soften slightly. Chop the chili and add with the cumin, coriander, and garlic. Cook a further 2-3 minutes. Add sugar, seasonings and tomatoes with their juice. Break up the tomatoes with a fork or a potato masher. Cook a further 5-6 minutes over moderate heat to reduce and thicken slighly. Add tomato paste for color, if necessary. Adjust seasoning and use hot or cold according to your recipe.

An indian woman selling baskets outside the cathedral in Zacatecas. The city's architectural beauty makes it a popular tourist resort.

Nachos

Preparation Time: about 25 minutes **Serves:** 8-10

These make excellent cocktail savories, and the variety of toppings and flavor combinations is almost endless.

Ingredients

1 package round tortilla chips
1 can refried beans
1 can Jalapeño bean dip
Full quantity Taco Sauce recipe
8-10 cherry tomatoes, sliced
½ cup sour cream or natural yogurt
Sliced black and stuffed green olives
Grated Cheddar cheese

Taco Filling
2 tsps oil
1 generous cup ground beef
2 tsps chili powder
Pinch ground coriander
Pinch cayenne pepper
Salt and pepper

Prepare taco filling as for Tacos recipe. Top half of the tortilla chips with refried beans and the remaining half with beef taco filling. Place a spoonful of taco sauce on the bean-topped chips and Jalapeño bean dip in the beef-topped chips. Top the tortilla chips with tomatoes, sour cream or yogurt, olives or cheese in any desired combination, and serve.

A Mexican couple give their *burro* a much needed rest.

Tacos

Preparation Time: 40 minutes **Cooking Time:** 15-20 minutes **Makes:** 12

Packaged taco shells make this famous Mexican snack easy to prepare, so spend the extra time on imaginative fillings.

Ingredients
12 taco shells

Beef Filling
1 tbsp oil
1lb ground beef
1 medium onion, chopped
2 tsps ground cumin
1 clove garlic, crushed
2 tsps chili powder
Pinch paprika
Salt and pepper

Chicken Filling
3 tbsps butter or margarine
1 medium onion, chopped
1 small red pepper, seeded
  and chopped
2 tbsps sliced almonds
12oz chicken breasts, skinned and
  finely chopped

Salt and pepper
1 piece fresh ginger, peeled
  and chopped
6 tbsps milk
2 tsps cornstarch
½ cup sour cream

Toppings
Shredded lettuce
Grated cheese
Tomatoes, seeded and chopped
Chopped green onions
Avocado slices
Sour cream
Jalapeño peppers
Taco sauce

Heat oil for the beef filling in a large frying pan and brown the beef and onions, breaking the meat up with a fork as it cooks. Add spices, garlic and seasoning and cook about 20 minutes. Set aside. Melt 2 tbsps butter or margarine in a medium saucepan and add the onion. Cook slowly until softened. Add the red pepper and almonds and cook slowly until the almonds are lightly browned. Stir often during cooking. Remove to a plate and set aside. Melt the remaining butter in the same saucepan and cook the chicken for about 5 minutes, turning frequently. Season and return the onion mixture to the pan along with the chopped ginger. Blend together the milk and cornstarch and stir into the chicken mixture. Bring to the boil and stir until very thick. Mix in the sour cream and cook gently to heat through. Do not boil. Heat the taco shells on a cookie sheet in a preheated oven at 350°F for 2-3 minutes. Place on the sheet with the open ends down.

To fill, hold the shell in one hand and spoon in about 1 tbsp of either beef or chicken filling. Next, add a layer of shredded lettuce, followed by a layer of grated cheese. Add choice of other toppings and finally spoon on some taco sauce.

Shrimp Veracruz

Preparation Time: about 25 minutes **Cooking Time:** about 15 minutes **Serves:** 6

Veracruz is a port on the Gulf of Mexico which lends its name to a variety of colorful seafood dishes.

Ingredients
1 tbsp oil
1 onion, chopped
1 large green pepper, cut into
   1½-inch strips
2-3 green chilies, seeded and
   chopped
Double quantity Taco Sauce recipe
2 tomatoes, skinned and roughly
   chopped

12 pimento-stuffed olives, halved
2 tsps capers
¼ tsp ground cumin
Salt
1lb shrimp, uncooked
Juice of 1 lime

Heat the oil in a large frying pan and add the onion and green pepper. Cook until soft but not colored. Add chilies, taco sauce, tomatoes, olives, capers, cumin and salt. Bring to the boil and then lower the heat to simmer for 5 minutes. Remove black veins, if present, from the rounded side of the shrimp with a wooden pick. Add the shrimp to the sauce and cook until they curl up and turn pink and opaque. Add the lime juice to taste and serve.

Top: a roadside vendor selling strawberries offers a welcome break for travelers.

Tostadas

Preparation Time: about 40 minutes **Cooking Time:** about 10-15 minutes
Makes: 12

These are popular all over Mexico and the toppings reflect the food available
in each area. They are delicious, but difficult to eat!

Ingredients	Toppings
2 tsps oil	Shredded lettuce
1lb ground beef or pork	Grated Cheddar cheese
2 tsps chili powder	Tomatoes, seeded and chopped
1 tsp ground cumin	Sour Cream
1 tsp ground coriander	Olives
1 can refried beans	Shrimp
1 package tostada shells	Taco sauce

Cook the meat in the oil in a medium frying pan. Sprinkle on the spices and
cook quickly to brown. Reheat the beans and place the tostada shells on a
baking sheet. Heat 2-3 minutes in a moderate oven. Spread 15-30ml/1-2
tbsps of the beans on each tostada shell. Top each shell with some of the
beef mixture.

Add the topping ingredients in different combinations and serve
immediately.

Top: colorful displays of chilies hang outside shops all over Mexico.

Chili Con Carne

Preparation Time: about 15 minutes **Cooking Time:** 25-30 minutes **Serves:** 4

Although this dish is Mexican in origin, the version everyone knows best is really more American.

Ingredients

1 tbsp oil
1lb ground beef
2 tsps ground cumin
2 tsps mild or hot chili powder
Pinch oregano

Salt, pepper and pinch sugar
¼ tsp garlic granules
2 tbsps flour
1lb canned tomatoes
1lb canned red kidney beans

Heat the oil in a large saucepan and brown the meat, breaking it up with a fork as it cooks. Sprinkle on the cumin, chili powder, oregano, salt, pepper, sugar, garlic and flour. Cook, stirring frequently, over medium heat for about 3 minutes. Add the tomatoes and their liquid and simmer 25-30 minutes. Drain the kidney beans and add just before serving. Heat through for about 5 minutes.

A potato chip vendor waits for custom in a busy shopping area in Zacatecas.

Burritos

Preparation Time: about 25 minutes **Cooking Time:** about 20 minutes **Serves:** 6

The name means "little donkeys" and the dish is a very popular one. Beans are the traditional filling, but meat may be used as well.

Ingredients

6 flour tortillas
1 onion, chopped
1 tbsp oil
1lb canned refried beans
6 lettuce leaves, shredded
2 tbsps snipped chives

2 tomatoes, sliced
1 cup Cheddar cheese, grated
Full quantity Taco Sauce recipe
½ cup sour cream
Chopped coriander leaves

Wrap tortillas in foil and heat in a warm oven to soften. Cook the onion in the oil until soft but not colored. Add the beans and heat through. Spoon the mixture down the center of each tortilla. Top with lettuce, cheese, tomatoes and chives. Fold over the sides to form long, rectangular parcel. Make sure the filling is completely enclosed. Place burritos in an ovenproof dish, cover and cook in a preheated 350°F oven for about 20 minutes.

Spoon over the taco sauce. Top with sour cream and sprinkle with chopped coriander to serve.

Picking cauliflowers for one of the markets which are held every Sunday.

Plaice in Spicy Tomato Sauce

Preparation Time: 30 minutes **Cooking Time:** 20-25 minutes **Serves:** 4

This piquant fish dish is popular along Mexico's Gulf coast. The sauce lends itself equally well to other varieties of fish, too.

Ingredients

3oz cream cheese
1 tsp dried oregano
Pinch cayenne pepper
4 whole fillets of plaice
Lime slices and dill to garnish

1 stick celery, chopped
1 chili pepper, seeded and chopped
¼ tsp each ground cumin, coriander and ginger
½ red and ½ green pepper, seeded and chopped

Tomato Sauce
1 tbsp oil
1 small onion, chopped

14oz canned tomatoes
1 tbsp tomato paste
Salt, pepper and a pinch sugar

Heat the oil in a heavy-based pan and cook the onion, celery, chili pepper and spices for about 5 minutes over very low heat. Add red and green peppers and the remaining sauce ingredients and bring to the boil. Reduce heat and simmer for 15-20 minutes, stirring occasionally. Set aside while preparing the fish. Mix the cream cheese, oregano and cayenne pepper together and set aside.

Skin the fillets using a filleting knife. Start at the tail end, holding the knife at a slight angle to the skin. Push the knife along using a sawing motion, with the blade against the skin. Dip fingers in salt to make it easier to grip the fish skin. Gradually separate the fish from the skin. Spread the cheese filling on all 4 fillets and roll each up. Secure with wooden picks. Place the fillets in a lightly greased baking dish, cover and cook for 10 minutes in a preheated 350°F oven. Pour over the tomato sauce and cook a further 10-15 minutes. The fish is cooked when it feels firm and looks opaque. Garnish with lime slices and dill.

Flautas

Preparation Time: about 1½ hours **Serves:** 6

Traditionally, these are long, thin rolls of tortillas with savory fillings, topped with sour cream.

Ingredients

8oz chicken, skinned, boned and ground or finely chopped
1 tbsp oil
1 small onion, finely chopped
½ green pepper, finely chopped
½-1 chili pepper, seeded and finely chopped
3oz frozen sweetcorn

6 black olives, pitted and chopped
½ cup heavy cream
Salt
12 prepared tortillas (see recipe for Flour Tortillas)
Taco sauce, guacamole and sour cream for toppings

Use a food processor or meat grinder to prepare the chicken, or chop by hand. Heat the oil in a medium frying pan and add the chicken, onion and green pepper. Cook over moderate heat, stirring frequently to break up the pieces of chicken. When the chicken is cooked and the vegetables are softened, add the chili, sweetcorn, olives, cream and salt. Bring to the boil over heat and boil rapidly, stirring continuously, to reduce and thicken the cream.

Place 2 tortillas on a clean work surface, overlapping them by about 2 inches. Spoon some of the chicken mixture onto the tortillas, roll up and secure with wooden picks. Fry the flautas in about ½ inch oil in a large frying pan. Do not allow the tortillas to get very brown. Drain on paper towels. Arrange flautas on serving plates and top with sour cream, guacamole and taco sauce.

Mexican Chicken and Pepper Salad

Preparation Time: about 30 minutes **Serves:** 6

This is the perfect lunch or light supper dish during the summer, and it can be prepared in advance.

Ingredients
1lb cooked chicken, cut in strips
½ cup mayonnaise
½ cup natural yogurt
1 tsp chili powder
1 tsp paprika
Pinch cayenne pepper
½ tsp tomato paste

1 tsp onion paste
1 green pepper, seeded and
  finely sliced
1 red pepper, seeded and
  finely sliced
6oz frozen sweetcorn, defrosted
6oz long-grain rice, cooked

Place the chicken strips in a large salad bowl. Mix the mayonnaise, yogurt, spices, tomato and onion pastes together and leave to stand briefly for flavors to blend. Fold dressing into the chicken. Add the peppers and sweetcorn and mix gently until all the ingredients are coated with dressing. Place the rice on a serving dish and pile the salad into the center. Serve immediately.

Top: Mexican rooftops are a strange mix of the traditional and the modern.

Chili Shrimp Quiche

Preparation Time: about 40 minutes **Cooking Time:** 30-40 minutes **Serves:** 6

Fresh chili peppers give a Mexican flavor to this quiche with its shrimp filling.

Ingredients

Pastry
1 cup all-purpose flour
Pinch salt
2 tbsps butter or margarine
2 tbsps white cooking fat
2-4 tbsps cold water

Filling
4 eggs
½ cup milk
½ cup light cream
½ clove garlic, crushed
1 cup grated Cheddar cheese
3 green onions, chopped
2 green chilies, seeded and chopped
1½ cups cooked and peeled shrimp
Salt
Cooked, unpeeled shrimp and
  parsley sprigs for garnish

Sift the flour with a pinch of salt into a mixing bowl, or place in a food processor and mix once or twice. Rub in the butter and fat until the mixture resembles fine breadcrumbs, or work in the food processor, being careful not to over-mix. Mix in the liquid gradually, adding enough to bring the pastry together into a ball. In a food processor, add the liquid through the funnel while the machine is running. Wrap the pastry well and chill for 20-30 minutes. Roll out the pastry on a well-floured surface with a floured rolling pin. Wrap the circle of pastry around the rolling pin to lift it into a 10-inch pie dish. Unroll the pastry over the dish. Carefully press the pastry into the bottom and up the sides of the dish, taking care not to stretch it. Roll the rolling pin over the top of the dish to remove excess pastry, or cut off with a sharp knife.

Mix the eggs, milk, cream and garlic together. Sprinkle the cheese, onion, chilies and shrimp onto the base of the pastry and pour over the egg mixture. Bake in a preheated 400°F oven for 30-40 minutes until firm and golden brown. Peel the tail shells off the shrimp and remove the legs and roe if present. Use to garnish the quiche along with the sprigs of parsley.

Empanadas

Preparation Time: about 30 minutes **Cooking Time:** about 35 minutes **Makes:** 6

Fillings for these turnovers can also be sweet. They are Spanish in origin and widely popular.

Ingredients

Triple quantity pastry recipe from
   Chili Shrimp Quiche
1 egg

Filling
1 onion, chopped
1 clove garlic, finely chopped
1 small green pepper, seeded
   and chopped
1 tbsp oil
1 generous cup ground beef

1 tsp cocoa powder
1 tbsp flour
½ tsp ground cumin
½ tsp paprika
½ tsp dried oregano, crushed
Salt and pepper
1-2 chilies, seeded and chopped
2 tbsps tomato paste
3 tbsps water
2 tbsps sliced almonds
2 tbsps raisins

Prepare the pastry according to the recipe for Chili Shrimp Quiche, or use packaged shortcrust pastry. Cook the onion, garlic and green pepper in the oil until soft but not colored. Add the meat and fry quickly until well browned. Add the cocoa, flour, spices, oregano, and seasonings, stir well and cook briefly before adding the chilies, tomato paste and water. Cook slowly for 10-15 minutes. Add almonds and raisins and allow to cool.

   Roll out the pastry on a floured surface and cut out 6 rounds using a 6-inch plate or saucepan lid as a guide. Place the cooled filling on one side of the rounds of pastry and dampen the edges with water. Fold over and press to seal the edges. Crimp the edges if desired. Place on baking sheets and brush with a mixture of beaten egg and salt. Make sure the egg glaze is brushed on evenly. Prick once or twice with a fork and bake at 425°F for about 15 minutes, or until golden brown.

Mexican Beef Patties

Preparation Time: about 20 minutes plus 1 hour chilling **Serves:** 4

Refried beans added to the meat mixture make moist and flavorsome beefburgers that are slightly out of the ordinary.

Ingredients
1 onion, finely chopped
1 tbsp oil
1½ cups ground beef
8oz canned refried beans
4 tbsps breadcrumbs
½ tsp cumin
1 tsp chili powder

1 clove garlic, crushed
Salt and pepper
1 egg, beaten
Flour to coat
Oil for frying
Watercress to garnish

Cook the onion in the oil until soft but not browned. Mix in the beef, beans, breadcrumbs, spices, garlic and seasoning and gradually add the egg until the mixture holds together well. Turn the mixture out onto a well-floured surface and divide into 8 pieces. Shape into even-sized patties with well-floured hands. Knead the pieces before shaping, if necessary, to make sure mixture holds together with no cracks. Coat lightly with flour and refrigerate until firm (approximately 1 hour).

Pour enough oil into a large frying pan to completely cover the patties. Fry 2 at a time until golden brown on all sides and completely cooked through. Remove from the oil and drain on paper towels. Arrange on a serving plate and garnish with watercress.

Top: Mexicans adore festivals such as this Saint's day celebration near Tabasco.

Albondigas

Preparation Time: about 25 minutes **Cooking Time:** about 20 minutes **Serves:** 4

A simple-to-make taco sauce makes these meatballs a lot less ordinary, and a lot more fun to eat.

Ingredients

1 generous cup ground veal
1 generous cup ground beef
1 clove garlic, crushed
2 tbsps dry breadcrumbs
½ chili pepper, seeded and
   finely chopped

½ tsp ground cumin
Salt and pepper
1 egg, beaten
Oil for frying
Full quantity Taco Sauce recipe
2 green onions, chopped

Mix together the veal, beef, garlic, breadcrumbs, chili pepper, cumin, salt and pepper until well blended. Add the egg gradually. Turn the mixture out onto a floured surface and divide into 16 equal pieces. With floured hands, shape the mixture into balls. Pour about 3 tbsps of oil into a large frying pan and place over high heat. When the oil is hot, place in the meatballs and fry for 5-10 minutes until brown on all sides. Turn frequently during cooking.

   Remove the browned meatballs and drain well on paper towels. Place in an ovenproof dish and pour over the taco sauce. Heat through in a preheated 350°F oven for 10 minutes. Sprinkle with chopped onions to serve.

A plethora of luxurious hotels service Mexico's blossoming tourist industry.

Chimichangas

Preparation Time: about 30 minutes **Cooking Time:** about 12-18 minutes **Serves:** 6

A strange sounding name for a delicious snack that is something like a deep-fried taco.

Ingredients
6 flour tortillas
Half quantity Chili Con Carne recipe
6 lettuce leaves, shredded
6 green onions, chopped
¾ cup grated Cheddar cheese

Oil for frying
Half quantity Guacamole recipe
½ cup sour cream
1 tomato, seeded and chopped

Wrap the tortillas in aluminum foil and place in a warm oven for 5 minutes to make them pliable. Heat the chili briefly and spoon about 2 tbsps onto the center of each tortilla. Top with lettuce, onions and cheese. Fold in the sides to make a parcel, making sure all the filling is enclosed.

Heat about 1 inch of oil in a large frying pan and when hot lower in the chimichangas, folded side down first. Cook 2-4 at a time depending on the size of the pan. Cook for 3 minutes and carefully turn over. Cook a further 3 minutes and remove to paper towels and drain. Repeat with remaining chimichangas.

Spoon the guacamole over the top of each, and drizzle over the sour cream. Sprinkle over the chopped tomato and serve immediately.

A fruit seller takes the chance for a refreshing break while the market is quiet.

Mexican Kebabs

Preparation Time: about 15 minutes **Cooking Time:** 25-30 minutes **Serves:** 4

Kebabs are a favorite barbecue food almost everywhere. The spice mixture and sauce give these their Mexican flavor.

Ingredients

1lb pork or lamb, cut into 2-inch pieces	¼ tsp garlic powder
4oz large button mushrooms, left whole	½ tsp dried marjoram
8 bay leaves	Salt and pepper
1 tsp cocoa powder	6 tbsps oil
2 tsps chili powder	2 medium onions, quartered
	6oz cooked rice
	½ quantity Taco Sauce recipe

Place meat and mushrooms in a bowl. Add the bay leaves, cocoa, chili powder, garlic powder, marjoram and seasoning to the oil and stir to coat all the ingredients with the marinade. Cover the bowl and leave to marinate at least 6 hours, preferably overnight. Remove meat, mushrooms and bay leaves from the marinade and reserve it. Thread onto skewers, alternating the meat, onions, mushrooms and bay leaves. Place under a preheated broiler for 15-20 minutes, turning frequently until cooked to desired degree. If using pork, the meat must be thoroughly cooked and not served pink. Baste with reserved marinade.

Mix hot rice with taco sauce, and spoon onto a warm serving dish. Place the kebabs on top of the rice to serve.

The fishing fleet awaits the early morning tide in Bacochibampo Bay, Guaymas.

Spare Ribs in Chili and Cream Sauce

Preparation Time: about 20 minutes **Cooking Time:** 50-55 minutes **Serves:** 4

Unsweetened cocoa lends color and depth to a sauce for ribs that's slightly more sophisticated than the usual barbecue sauce.

Ingredients

2¼lbs spare ribs
1 tsp cocoa powder
1 tbsp flour
½ tsp cumin
½ tsp paprika
½ tsp dried oregano, crushed

Salt and pepper
1 cup warm water
2 tbsps thin honey
2 tbsps heavy cream
Lime wedges and watercress
   for garnish

Leave the ribs in whole slabs and roast at 400°F for 20-25 minutes, or until well browned. Drain off all the excess fat.

Blend together the cocoa, flour, cumin, paprika, oregano, seasoning, water and honey and pour over the ribs. Lower the temperature to 350°F and cook ribs for a further 30 minutes, until the sauce has reduced and the ribs are tender. Cut the ribs into pieces and arrange on a serving dish. Pour the cream into the sauce in the roasting pan and place over moderate heat. Bring to the boil and pour over the ribs. Garnish with lime wedges and serve.

Top: a tortilla factory displays all the color of Mexico's folk art traditions.

Enchiladas

Preparation Time: about 1½ hours **Serves:** 6

Although fillings and sauces vary, enchiladas are one of the tastiest Mexican dishes.

Ingredients

10 ripe tomatoes, peeled, seeded and chopped
1 small onion, chopped
1-2 green or red chilies, seeded and chopped
1 clove garlic, crushed
Salt
Pinch sugar
1-2 tbsps tomato paste
2 tbsps butter or margarine
2 eggs
1 cup heavy cream
4 tbsps grated cheese
1½ cups ground pork
1 small red pepper, seeded and chopped
4 tbsps raisins
4 tbsps pine nuts
Salt and pepper
12 prepared tortillas (see recipe for Flour Tortillas)
Sliced green onions to garnish

Place tomatoes, onion, chilies, garlic, salt and sugar in a blender or food processor and blend until smooth. Melt butter or margarine in a large saucepan. Add the blended tomatoes and simmer for 5 minutes. Beat together the eggs and cream, mixing well. Add a spoonful of the hot tomato paste to the cream and eggs and mix quickly. Return mixture to the saucepan with the rest of the tomato paste. Reserve cheese for topping. Heat slowly, stirring constantly, until the mixture thickens. Do not boil.

While preparing the sauce, cook the pork and pepper slowly in a large frying pan. Use a fork to break up the meat as it cooks. Raise the heat when the pork is nearly cooked and fry briskly for a few minutes. Add the raisins, pine nuts and seasoning. Combine about ¼ of the sauce with the meat and divide mixture evenly among all the tortillas. Spoon on the filling to one side of the center and roll up the tortilla around it, leaving the ends open and some of the filling showing.

Place enchiladas seam side down in a baking pan and pour over the remaining sauce, leaving the ends uncovered. Sprinkle over the cheese and bake in a preheated 350°F oven for 15-20 minutes, or until the sauce begins to bubble. Sprinkle with the sliced onions and serve immediately.

Minute Steaks with Taco Sauce

Preparation Time: about 15 minutes **Cooking Time:** 15-20 minutes **Serves:** 6

A quick meal needn't be ordinary. Prepare taco sauce ahead and keep it on hand to add last-minute spice to a meal.

Ingredients

Full quantity Taco Sauce recipe
2 tbsps butter or margarine
2 tbsps oil
6 minute steaks

Salt and pepper
4oz button mushrooms, left whole
Chopped parsley or coriander leaves

Prepare taco sauce according to the recipe directions. Heat the butter or margarine and oil together in a large frying or sauté pan. Season the steaks with salt and pepper and fry 2 or 3 at a time for 2-3 minutes on each side, or to desired degree.

Remove the steaks to a warm serving dish and add the mushrooms to the pan. Sauté over high heat to brown lightly, remove and keep warm. Drain most of the fat from the pan and pour in the taco sauce. Place over low heat until just bubbling. Spoon the sauce over the steaks. Top the steaks with the sautéed mushrooms and sprinkle over parsley or coriander before serving.

Top: early evening in Mexico's restaurants is a time for coffee or cocktails.

Leg of Lamb with Chili Sauce

Preparation Time: about 15 minutes **Cooking Time:** about 2 hours for the lamb and 20 minutes to finish the sauce **Serves:** 4

Give Sunday roast lamb a completely different taste with a spicy orange sauce.

Ingredients
2¼lb leg of lamb

Marinade
1 tsp cocoa powder
¼ tsp cayenne pepper
½ tsp ground cumin
½ tsp paprika
½ tsp ground oregano
½ cup water

½ cup orange juice
½ cup red wine
1 clove of garlic, crushed
2 tbsps brown sugar
1 tbsp cornstarch
Pinch salt
Orange slices and coriander
   to garnish

If the lamb has a lot of surface fat, trim slightly with a sharp knife. If possible, remove the paper-thin skin on the outside of the lamb. Place lamb in a shallow dish.

Mix together the marinade ingredients, except cornstarch and garnishes, and pour over the lamb, turning it well to coat completely. Cover and refrigerate for 12-24 hours, turning occasionally. Drain the lamb, reserving the marinade, and place in a roasting pan. Cook in a preheated 350°F oven for about 2 hours, until meat is cooked according to taste. Baste occasionally with the marinade and pan juices. Remove lamb to a serving dish and keep warm. Skim the fat from the top of the roasting pan with a large spoon and discard. Pour remaining marinade into the pan juices in the roasting pan and bring to the boil, stirring to loosen the sediment. Mix cornstarch with a small amount of water and add some of the liquid from the roasting pan. Gradually stir cornstarch mixture into the pan and bring back to the boil. Cook, stirring constantly, until thickened and clear. Add more orange juice, wine or water as necessary. Garnish the lamb with orange slices and sprigs of coriander. Pour over some of the sauce and serve the rest separately.

Mango Fool

Preparation Time: about 20 minutes **Serves:** 6

A mixture of mango, lime, ginger and cream is the perfect way to cool the palate after a spicy Mexican meal.

Ingredients
2 ripe mangoes
1 small piece fresh ginger, peeled
  and shredded

1 cup sifted confectioner's sugar
Juice of ½ a lime
1 cup heavy cream

Cut the mangoes in half, cutting around the stone. Scoop the pulp into a bowl, blender or food processor. Reserve two slices. Add the ginger, confectioner's sugar and lime juice and blend until smooth. Use a hand blender or electric mixer in the bowl, pushing mixture through a sieve afterwards, if necessary. Whip the cream until soft peaks form and fold into the mango purée. Divide the mixture between 6 glass serving dishes and leave in the refrigerator for 1 hour before serving. Cut the reserved mango slices into 6 smaller slices or pieces and use these to garnish.

A whole range of products tempt the passing motorists on Mexico's highways.

Tropical Fruit Salad

Preparation Time: about 45 minutes **Serves:** 6

A refreshing mixture of exotic fruits is the most popular dessert in Mexico. Add tequila or triple sec to the syrup for a special occasion.

Ingredients

½ cantaloup or honeydew melon, cubed or made into balls
½ small fresh pineapple, peeled, cored and cubed or sliced
4oz fresh strawberries, hulled and halved (leave whole if small)
1 mango, peeled and sliced or cubed
8oz watermelon, seeded and cubed
4oz guava or papaya, peeled and cubed

2 oranges, peeled and segmented
1 prickly pear, peeled and sliced (optional)
½ cup sugar
½ cup water
Grated rind and juice of 1 lemon
2 tbsps chopped pecans to garnish (optional)

To make melon balls, cut melons in half, scoop out seeds and discard them. Press the cutting edge of the melon baller firmly into the melon flesh and twist around to scoop out round pieces. It is easy to core the pineapple if it is first cut into quarters. Use a serrated fruit knife to cut the point off the quarter, removing the core. Slice off the peel. Cut into slices or cubes and mix with the other fruit. Dissolve the sugar in the water over gentle heat and, when the mixture is no longer grainy, leave it to cool completely. Add lemon rind and juice to the sugar syrup and pour over the prepared fruit. Refrigerate well before serving. Sprinkle with chopped nuts, if desired.

Top: a fruit market stays open to catch the last few late-night shoppers.

Mexican Chocolate Flan

Preparation Time: about 30 minutes **Cooking Time:** about 35-40 minutes **Serves:** 4

Flan in Mexico is a molded custard with a caramel sauce. Chocolate and cinnamon is a favorite flavor combination.

Ingredients

½ cup sugar
2 tbsps water
Juice of ½ a lemon
1 cup milk
2oz semi-sweet chocolate

1 cinnamon stick
2 whole eggs
2 egg yolks
4 tbsps sugar

Combine the first amount of sugar with the water and lemon juice in a small, heavy-based saucepan. Cook over gentle heat until the sugar starts to dissolve. Swirl the pan from time to time, but do not stir. Once the sugar liquifies, bring the syrup to the boil and cook until golden brown.

While preparing the syrup, heat 4 custard cups in a 350°F oven. When the syrup is ready, pour into the dishes and swirl to coat the sides and base evenly. Leave to cool at room temperature. Chop the chocolate into small pieces and heat with the milk and cinnamon, stirring occasionally to help chocolate dissolve. Whisk the whole eggs and the yolks together with the remaining sugar until slightly frothy. Gradually whisk in the chocolate milk. Remove cinnamon stick. Pour the chocolate custard carefully into the custard cups and place them in a roasting pan of hand-hot water.

Place the roasting pan in the oven and bake the custards until just slightly wobbly in the center, about 20-30 minutes. Cool at room temperature and refrigerate for several hours or overnight before serving. Loosen custards carefully from the sides of the dishes and invert into serving plates. Shake to allow custard to drop out.

Tequila Sunrise

Serves: 4

Ingredients

½ cup tequila
1½ cups orange juice
4 tbsps Cointreau or Grand Marnier

Ice
4 tbsps Grenadine syrup

Crush the ice, place in a blender with the tequila, orange juice and orange liqueur and mix thoroughly. Chill 4 tall glasses in the refrigerator and when cold, pour in the cocktail mixture. Hold each glass at a tilt and carefully pour 1 tbsp Grenadine syrup down one side. The syrup will sink to the bottom giving the drink its sunrise effect.

Margarita

Serves: 2

Tequila drinks are unmistakably Mexican. They are deceptive – pleasant to sip but with quite a kick!

Ingredients

1 lime
Coarse salt
½ cup tequila

2 tbsps triple sec
4 ice cubes

Squeeze the lime and moisten the rim of two cocktail glasses with a small amount of juice. Pour salt onto a plate and dip in the moistened rims of the glasses, turning to coat evenly. Refrigerate to chill thoroughly. Crush 4 ice cubes and place in a blender with the tequila and triple sec. Blend until slushy. Pour into the chilled glasses and serve immediately.